Mission Possible

Enhancing Nonprofit Communication for Optimum Impact

Table of Contents

Chapter 1. Introduction

In the modern era of increasing digitalization and competition for resources, effective communication has become the lifeblood for nonprofit organizations to reach their goals and make a difference. Our Special Report, titled "Mission Possible: Enhancing Nonprofit Communication for Optimum Impact," uncovers the secrets of successful nonprofit communication strategies and delivers a comprehensive guide to maximize your organization's reach and potential impact. This report is teeming with valuable insights, data-driven strategies, and proven methodologies to transform your messages into powerful tools for change. Whether you are a new nonprofit struggling to get your voice heard or an established entity aiming to further amplify your impact, you'll surely find this report a treasure-trove of practical advice woven with inspiring success stories. Get ready to make your mission possible, one effective communication at a time!

Chapter 2. Translating Vision into Words: Crafting a Compelling Nonprofit Story

At the heart of every successful nonprofit organization is a compelling story - a story that conveys its vision, resonates with its audiences, and inspires action. This story, when crafted well, can become your organization's most powerful tool for engagement.

2.1. Understand Your Vision

At its core, your nonprofit's story should reflect its vision. But before you can begin crafting that story, it is imperative to have a thorough understanding of what that vision is. What is your organization's mission, what are its goals, and what does it hope to achieve in the long run?

Begin by defining your vision succinctly and clearly. What is the purpose your organization exists to serve? What problem are you trying to solve? Where do you see your organization in the next five or ten years? Think big, but also make sure your vision is achievable. Remember, vague goals breed vague results. Having a clear vision is key to creating an engaging story that does justice to your organization's ideals and aspirations.

2.2. Emphasize Your Unique Value Proposition

What sets your organization apart from others in the same domain? Why should someone support your cause over another? Your uniqueness or 'differentiator' can be an extremely powerful tool to entice your audience. Your unique value proposition (UVP) could be anything from a unique approach to a problem, a compelling origin story, or a distinctive way of engaging with your community.

Highlighting your UVP in your nonprofit's story can help enhance your credibility and build trust among potential donors, volunteers, and advocates. It gives them a reason to believe in your cause and assures them that their support can make a unique and significant impact.

2.3. Use Emotive Narratives

Once you have your vision and UVP clear, it's time to start crafting your story. An effective nonprofit story is one that connects emotionally with an audience. To achieve this, you need to weave emotive narratives into your story. Consider the following strategies:

Highlight Personal Stories: Rather than focusing solely on statistics and general goals, bring your narrative to life with personal stories. These could be success stories of individuals or communities your organization has served, tales of struggles and triumphs among your team, or testimonials from volunteers and donors illustrating their connection to your cause.

Leverage the Power of Visuals: A picture is worth a thousand words, and it holds particularly true when trying to convey emotion. Consider including photographs, infographics, or short videos in your narratives to amplify the emotional subtext.

Use Vivid Descriptions: Engage your audience's senses by using vivid and descriptive language when telling personal stories or explaining your mission and goals.

2.4. Mastering Your Storytelling Methods

Knowing your story is important, but equally significant is knowing how to tell your story. Different stories require different treatments, and your method should be guided by your audience, your medium, and your desired outcome.

Written Content: Thorough, heartfelt, and well-crafted written content that covers your journey, impact, and vision can be a powerful tool for blogs, newsletters, reports, and website copy. Utilize compelling headlines, gripping introductions, and impactful conclusions.

Video Storytelling: Video is a potent way to reach and engage audiences, clearly convey messages, and create emotional connections. Keep them short, highly visual, and full of emotions.

Social Media: Social media platforms provide a great opportunity to reach a large and diverse audience. Create bite-sized content that is eye-catching, easily consumable, and shareable.

2.5. Wrapping Up: Review and Revise

Once you have crafted what you feel is a compelling story, take a step back and review it. Read it from your audience's perspective. Is it engaging from start to end? Is it clear, concise, and compelling? Does it effectively communicate your vision and the difference your organization is making?

Ask for feedback from individuals both within and outside of your organization. This can provide invaluable perspectives and suggestions for improvements that you may not have identified.

After making any needed revisions, your story is ready to be shared. Invest in appropriate channels of communication to ensure your compelling story is heard, understood, and has the impact it deserves.

Good story crafting and effective storytelling are not learnt overnight. It's an ongoing process, one that evolves with your organization, its growth and the change it effects. Remember, every evolution of your organization's journey is a new chapter of your story waiting to be told. Make it memorable, make it inspiring, and most importantly, make it your own.

Chapter 3. Understanding Your Audience: Insights and Strategies

In order to communicate effectively, it is crucial that we first understand who we are talking to. Hence, recognizing your audience demographic is the cornerstone of every successful communication strategy, particularly for nonprofits aiming to make a significant change. This section emphasizes the significance of identifying who your audience is and presents you with an array of practical strategies and insightful data-driven means to successful audience comprehension.

3.1. The Importance of Understanding Your Audience

Understanding your audience is a fundamental aspect of communication. If the audience fails to connect with the message, your efforts can be rendered futile. This is not only because the content might not be appealing or relevant to them but also owing to the fact that it could have been delivered at an inappropriate time or through an unsuitable channel. Understanding your audience therefore can help your nonprofit to:

- Reduce resource wastage by focusing on the right channels for communication

- Improve message engagement by tailoring content to suit their preferences

- Better anticipate audience needs, expectations and behaviors

- Enhance the reach of your messages and amplify the impact

3.2. Recognizing Your Audience

You will often find that your work leads you to connect with a variety of audience groups - beneficiaries, donors, volunteers, community leaders, and even policymakers. Each group will have distinct characteristics, needs, and communication preferences which you need to consider. There are several ways to identify these groups:

- Donor data analysis: Looking at historical trends in your donations can help you understand who your key supporters are and what influences their decisions to give.

- Beneficiary surveys: Directly engaging with those you serve can give you insights into their unique needs and how best to connect with them.

- Volunteer tracking: Your volunteers are often an untapped source of rich insights. Fostering engagement could help glean insights into their demographics, motivations, and preferences.

- Stakeholder Interviews: Conversations with community leaders and policymakers can help you understand their individual perspectives and preferences.

You should cluster these groups based on shared characteristics or needs. For instance, the primary groups could be existing donors, potential donors, local community organizations, partner agencies, and program recipients. These primary groups can then be broken down into smaller segments, offering a more personalized approach to their communication needs.

3.3. Unleashing the Power of Data

Inside the guise of multiple spreadsheets, CRM databases, and social media metrics, there lies a treasure trove of data that nonprofits can utilize to understand their audiences better. Here's how:

- Quantitative data: This numerical data can help you track trends, measure impact, and identify patterns. This might include data such as the number of active volunteers, demographic breakdown of donors, or the number of beneficiaries served in a particular timeframe.

- Qualitative data: This type of data gives context to your numbers. In-depth interviews, case studies, open-ended survey responses – all these provide deeper insights into your audience's needs, motivations, and preferences.

- Social media analytics: These can often provide real-time insights into how your audience interacts with your content. Which posts are they sharing? What comments are they leaving? These insights can offer valuable guidance for your communication strategy.

Don't forget to follow ethical guidelines when dealing with data, respect people's privacy and confidentiality, and always ask for consent where necessary.

3.4. Developing Persona Profiles

Based on your data analysis, it can be useful to develop persona profiles. These are detailed representations of your ideal audience segments that include demographics, behavior patterns, motivations, and goals. Persona profiles allow you to visualize your audience and personalize your content effectively.

To develop a persona:

1. Identify key demographic details

2. Understand their motivations, needs, communication preferences, and challenges.

3. Detail out their behavior patterns and lifestyle.

4. Keep personas realistic, relatable, and limited to avoid

stereotypes.

The more detailed they are, the more accurately they represent your audience, leading to more effective strategies.

3.5. Evaluating and Adapting

None of this is a one-off process. People evolve, trends shift, and your nonprofit must adapt. Regular review and analysis of your data and strategies are critical to ensure that your communication continues to hit the mark. Stay open to change, be responsive to feedback, and be willing to test new approaches. It can be valuable to undertake a regular audience analysis and revisit your persona profiles.

Understanding your audience is the first step in effective communication. By following the strategies outlined in this chapter, you can make informed decisions tailored to your audience, paving the way for stronger relationships and greater impact. Remember, communication is not about talking to the masses, but about talking to individuals - Understanding them is your first mission towards your larger goal.

Chapter 4. Digital Communication: Harnessing the Power of Social Media for Nonprofits

In today's interconnected world, digital communication and, in particular, social media have revolutionized the way nonprofits engage with their constituents, share their vision, and rally support for their cause. The power and potential of these platforms can effectively be harnessed to enhance the reach and impact of your organization.

4.1. The Rise of Social Media: A Game-Changer

The advent of social media has significantly altered the communication landscape. It has democratized content creation and distribution, empowering organizations of all sizes to tell their stories, connect with supporters, inspire action, and promote advocacy. The Pew Research Center reports as of 2021, roughly 72% of the American public uses social media. This near ubiquity makes it a powerful tool for nonprofits to leverage for optimum impact. However, to exploit its full potential, understanding its nuances, strengths, and limitations is crucial.

4.2. Understanding Different Social Media Platforms

There are several social media platforms, each catering to a different demographic and offering unique features. Some of the most popular ones are Facebook, Twitter, Instagram, LinkedIn, and YouTube. To craft a successful social media strategy, your nonprofit should choose platforms that best align with your target audience's demographics and behavioral patterns.

Facebook, with over 2.8 billion monthly active users, is known for its broad demographic reach. It's great for sharing updates, posting event details, and promoting fundraising campaigns. Twitter is ideal for instant communication, gaining insights into trending topics and promoting dialogue through hashtags. Instagram, characterized by its visual-driven interface, lends itself well to sharing powerful images and stories. LinkedIn is a professional network suitable for thought leadership, hiring, and B2B relationships. YouTube is a video-sharing platform where organizations can share in-depth storytelling through video content.

4.3. Constructing a Strategic Social Media Plan

Just like any other organizational task, successful social media engagement also requires careful planning. This involves setting clear objectives, identifying your target audience, curating appropriate content, timing your posts effectively, and analyzing the results regularly.

In the objectives, be as precise as possible — driving website traffic, raising funds, recruiting volunteers, or increasing event attendance could be some goals. Knowing your audience is crucial for curating resonating content and choosing the right platforms. Use demographic data to inform your decisions.

Maintain a consistent voice across all platforms, reflecting your nonprofit's values, ethos, and vision. Visual content, real-life stories, and user-generated content work well on these channels.

4.4. Engagement: The Key to Social Media Success

Social media is not just about broadcasting information; it's about fostering engagement. Encourage two-way dialogue with your followers by posing questions, responding to comments, and celebrating your supporters. This interactive dialogue will build a loyal community that feels valued and connected to your cause.

4.5. Leveraging Social Media for Fundraising

Social media serves as an effective fundraising tool. You can use platforms to reach out to donors, share fundraising campaigns, and update supporters about the impact of their donations. Facebook's fundraising tool, for instance, allows nonprofits to raise funds directly from the platform.

4.6. Analytics: Measuring Success and Refining Strategy

Track your social media performance regularly using the analytics tools provided by the platforms. Metrics like reach, engagement, and conversions provide insight into what is working and what isn't, aiding in the refinement of your strategy.

4.7. Social Media Compliance: Staying on the Right Side of the Law

When using social media, it's essential to be aware of the legalities that come with it. Avoid misrepresentation, respect copyright and privacy laws, and ensure any marketing communication complies with the necessary legal regulations.

4.8. Looking Ahead: Social Media's Evolving Role

Like all digital technology, social media is constantly evolving. Nonprofits must stay current with these changes to continue reaping its benefits. Whether it's new algorithms, feature rollouts, or emerging platforms, staying up-to-date ensures your nonprofit will continue to thrive in the digital realm.

In conclusion, with careful planning and execution, social media can be a powerful tool in furthering the goals of your nonprofit. By fostering genuine connections with your audience, you can build a loyal community that champions your cause, mobilizing a network of supporters that's larger and more engaged than ever before. Harnessing the power of social media is truly making the mission possible, one post, one like, and one share at a time.

Chapter 5. Press Releases and Newsletters: Leveraging Traditional Media

In a world where digital and social media command attention, traditional media – press releases and newsletters – might seem regrettably out of sync. However, they remain critically important and effective tools in the nonprofit communication belt. Leveraging these tools can bring your cause to the forefront, delivering your messages right to your connecters' antennae – the journalists, bloggers, niche publishers, community leaders, who can amplify your voice.

5.1. The Power of Press Releases

Press releases are official statements written for distribution to news media. The goal: to spread your organization's message, milestone, or event as widely as possible.

A Primer on Press Release Writing

A press release should answer the 5W1H: Who, What, Where, When, Why, and How. Write it like a news report with the most important information first followed by details, in descending order of significance - a technique known as 'Inverted Pyramid.'

Keep it concise, staying between 400 and 500 words. Use professional language, but make sure it's accessible to the average reader. Include quotes from relevant stakeholders for authenticity, and incorporate the right keywords to optimize for SEO.

Restorative Justice Forum Illustration

e.g., Restituo, a nonprofit fighting for reforms in justice, recently held a 'Restorative Justice Forum.'

The press release title was "Restituo's Restorative Justice Forum Paves Path to a More Empathetic Legal System." It combined the key message with an enticing headline using appropriate keywords.

5.2. The Distribution of Press Releases

Making your press release is only half the battle. You must put your release into the right hands to get your news picked up.

Build Relationships with Journalists

Develop a preferred-contacts list of journalists who cover areas related to your mission. Send personalized emails with your press releases.

Attend Networking Events

Networking events can provide opportunities to meet journalists in-person. Maintain contact by engaging in conversations, sharing ideas, and most importantly, through regular post-event follow-ups.

Use PR Distribution Services

PR distribution services, like PR Newswire or PRWeb, help effectively distribute your press releases. There can be costs associated, but they can help reach a broader audience.

5.3. Understanding Newsletters

Newsletters help maintain an organization's tie with its community, donors, volunteers, and service recipients. They deliver updates, stories, events, achievements, and requests directly to interested parties.

Match your newsletter's design to your brand. Be consistent with colors, fonts, and layout. Use high-quality images to break up text and make it engaging, and try to keep it concise.

Your newsletter should focus on your audience's interests. Share success stories, profile volunteers, staff or service recipients, and provide updates on your work. Remember to use compelling headlines, bullet points and short paragraphs to maintain reader's interest.

5.4. Deploying Newsletters

Target the Right Audience

Maintain a database of contacts to send your newsletters. Identify groups within your subscribers – such as donors, volunteers, and service recipients – and consider personalizing some content for these subgroups for more impact.

Email or Direct Mail?

The method of distribution depends on your audience's preferences and your resources. Direct mail can be expensive but is sometimes more effective for less tech-savvy audiences. Email is more economical and widespread but can struggle with open rates. A mix of both according to different audience preferences can be an effective strategy.

Conclusion

In conclusion, while digitization propels us towards new means of communication at rapid paces, traditional media – press releases and newsletters – still hold ample power in getting the word out effectively about your nonprofit's mission and activities. It's crucial to remember the basic tenets of relatability, personalization, and relevance, no matter what platform you choose to use. With the correct application of these tools, your organization can continue to make strides in realizing its goals, reinforcing its messages, and maintaining a genuine connection with its audience. After all, your impact is only as effective as your communication.

Chapter 6. Creating Engaging Content: A Guide for Nonprofits

The non-profit sector has matured into a dynamic milieu of organizations that are constantly trying to convey their causes to stakeholders amidst the cacophony of digital media traffic. With the advancement of technology, the channels for communication have broadened but so have the challenges of getting your voice heard. One powerful tool that continues to break barriers is engaging content. Interesting, compelling, and accessible content often forms the crux of your non-profit's voice, helping it reverberate across donor communities, volunteers, beneficiaries, and the wider public.

6.1. Understanding Your Audience

Before you start churning out content, it's imperative to know to whom you are speaking. Understanding your audience allows you to tailor your messages to their needs, preferences, and behaviors. Start by finding answers to questions such as who are they, what are they interested in, and how do they prefer to consume content. Create audience personas to help you visualize your target audience. Each persona can stand for a different segment of your audience – donors, volunteers, or beneficiaries.

6.2. Crafting Your Message

Once you have developed a clear understanding of your audience, you can start crafting your message. Ensure that your message aligns with your organization's mission and conveys the impact you are creating in the community or on the cause you are addressing. This aspect of content creation calls for a balance between emotional storytelling and factual representation. Show real-life stories of impact and success but also include data to validate the change your non-profit is driving.

6.3. Choosing the Right Content Format

Different types of content speak to different groups of people. Articles, videos, infographics, podcasts, webinars, social media posts can all be effective at conveying your message, but your choice should be tailored to your audience's preferences. Use audience personas to identify which format would be most successful for each segment. For example, younger audiences may be more influenced by visual content, while older audiences might prefer detailed reports and articles.

6.4. Techniques for Audience Engagement

There are several strategies that nonprofits can use to increase engagement with their content. These strategies include using actionable language, incorporating visuals, and leveraging interactive content.

1. Actionable language: Use language that encourages your audience to take action. Actionable language not only imparts urgency to your message but also encourages your audience to contribute to your cause in tangible ways.

2. Incorporating visuals: Use images, infographics, and videos to make your content more engaging. Visuals can express complex ideas quickly and effectively, making your content easier to digest and share.

3. Interactive content: Content types like quizzes, surveys, polls can

be a great way to involve your audience actively in your cause. They create a two-way dialog, improve engagement, and provide valuable data.

6.5. Leverage Social Media

Social media is a powerful tool for all types of content sharing, whether it's articles, pictures, or video. Be aware of the different strengths of each platform. Facebook is better for detailed posts and community building, Instagram for visual content, LinkedIn for professional and networking oriented content, and Twitter for bite-sized updates and discussions. Use your content to tell stories, engage audiences, and create conversations around your cause.

6.6. Content Evaluation and Improvement

Content creation for nonprofits is not a one-time effort, but a continuous process. It's important to regularly evaluate the effectiveness of your content and adjust your strategy accordingly. Use analytics tools to track engagement and gain insight into what content resonates the most with your audience. This feedback loop will serve as a guide in refining your content production and distribution strategies.

Remember the power of engaging content - it invites participation, drives action, and fosters a deeper connection with your cause. With diligence and creativity, your organization can create content that not only informs and inspires but also propels your mission forward.

Chapter 7. Communication Strategies for Fundraising Success

Fundraising is an integral part of a nonprofit's life cycle that enables it to realize its mission and objectives successfully. It hinges heavily on the potency of the communication strategies employed. Effective communication serves to enlighten prospective donors about the nonprofit's cause, cement trust, and inspire them to donate generously. The success of a fundraising campaign starkly depends on how effectively the nonprofit communicates.

7.1. Understanding Your Audience

Before developing any communication strategy, it's crucial to comprehensively understand your audience. Who are they? What motivates them to donate? How do they prefer to be contacted?

Borrowing tools from market research, such as surveys and focus groups, can glean invaluable information about your audience's preferences, motivations, and behaviors. Use this data to segment your audience into different groups based on these factors. Segmentation aids in tailoring communication to resonate deeply with each.

Remember, one-size-fits-all communication doesn't work effectively. Personalize your messages to meet the unique considerations of each audience group; this will boost their interest and desire to contribute.

7.2. Crafting Your Message

Once you've gained a clear understanding of your audience, the next step is to craft your message. Your goal is to create a compelling narrative that deeply connects the audience with your cause.

Make it clear about what you're raising funds for. The purpose of the campaign must be communicated effectively. Where will the funds go, and how they will be used? Transparency boosts donor trust, which can culminate in more generous donations.

Bring your story to life by incorporating voices from those your organization serves. Personal stories about how your organization has made or is making a difference can be very compelling. A good story can inspire, connect, and encourage your audience to take action.

7.3. Choosing a Communication Medium

Today, nonprofits have a multitude of communication channels to choose from: direct mail, email, social media, website updates, newsletters, personal calls, webinars, events, among many others. It's vital to select a medium that best aligns with your audience's preferences.

For instance, the older audience may prefer direct mail or personal calls, while younger patrons may be more responsive to digital forms of communication such as email, website content, or social media updates. Thus, picking the effective communication channel is as crucial as crafting a persuasive message.

7.4. Leveraging Storytelling in Fundraising

People love a good story; they're wired to respond to them. Nonprofits can leverage storytelling to create an emotional connection with their potential donors.

The story should start with a problem that your organization aims to solve, providing context and rationale for your mission. It should then introduce an individual or a group that benefits directly from your organization's work, taking the audience on a journey of transformation. A powerful story creates a sense of urgency and importance around your cause, motivating individuals to become a part of your mission.

7.5. Timing is Crucial

In fundraising, timing can be critical. The right message at the right time can significantly enhance your campaign's effectiveness. Research shows that certain times of the year, such as holiday seasons, prompt more charitable donations. Thus, aligning your appeals with these times can increase the likelihood of contributions.

But don't limit yourself to only these seasons. Regular communication throughout the year is crucial as it helps keep your cause at the forefront of your audience's minds.

7.6. Measuring Success and Learning from Failures

Lastly, it's essential to track the results of your communication strategies and learn from them. Consider implementing donation tracking software to gain insights into donor behavior and preferences.

Use those data and feedback to evaluate the effectiveness of your efforts. Discover what worked and what didn't. Is there something you could do differently? Are there new strategies you could incorporate? Continuous learning and adaptation should form the core of your communication strategy.

In conclusion, communication strategy is integral for fundraising success. By understanding your audience, crafting compelling messages, careful selection of communication channels and timing, not only can you reach your fundraising goals, but you also create a community of donors who are invested in your cause and its success.

Chapter 8. Multimedia Communication: From Concept to Execution

As we journey through this digital era, it's imperative for nonprofit organizations to embrace a robust and effective multimedia communication. This reciprocal exchange, facilitated by various media types such as text, graphics, audio, and video, holds the power to boost your organization's credibility and reach.

8.1. Understanding Multimedia Communication

Multimedia communication is a combination of at least two or more communication types, combining text, audio, graphics, and video to create a more engaging, interactive, and effective communication method. This interactive mode of communication is extensively employed in numerous fields such as entertainment, business, and in our case, nonprofit organizations.

As nonprofits move away from the traditional forms of communication like newsletters and event invitations, multimedia becomes a crucial tool in promoting their missions on digital platforms. Their ability to effectively leverage this resource can significantly enhance their reach, engagement, and ultimately their impact.

8.2. Significance of Multimedia Communication In Nonprofits

Nonprofit organizations often grapple with limited resources, making it even more crucial for their messaging to be impactful and reach their right audience. With multimedia content, they can narrate their stories in an immersive and engaging manner, prompting better response and participation from audiences.

- Interactive Content: Multimedia communication allows nonprofits to create interactive and engaging content, compelling viewers to lean in and actively participate.

- Diverse Communication Opportunities: With multimedia, a nonprofit is not restricted to one form of communication. The use of images, sound, and video adds depth to the narrative, creating a more impactful story.

- Emotional Connection: Multimedia content can help nonprofits establish a deeper emotional connect with their audience. This can be critical when trying to raise awareness or funds.

- Reach Wider Audiences: By including videos, infographics, and more into their content strategy, nonprofits can engage multiple senses, making content more memorable and increasing the potential audience range.

8.3. Creating An Effective Multimedia Communication Strategy

Creating an effective multimedia communication strategy is a systematic and thoughtful process. It requires a deep understanding of your organization, audience, and the message you want to channel.

- Understand Your Audience: Conduct regular surveys and interviews to gauge your audience's interests and the type of content they engage with. This can guide your multimedia content creation.

- Leverage Different Forms Of Media: Variety can prevent your content from becoming stale and predictable. Test out various media types to see what works best with your audience.

- Consistency in Message: Ensure that your multimedia content consistently aligns with your organization's mission and values. This strengthens your brand image and promulgates credibility.

- Make Content Shareable: The more your content is shared, the wider it reaches. Design content that your audience will want to share on their channels.

8.4. Implementing Multimedia Communication Strategy

Now that you have crafted an effective multimedia communication strategy, it's time to execute it.

- Quality Over Quantity: While it's essential to keep your audience engaged, focus on the quality of your content. Poorly constructed content can cause more harm than good.

- Flexibility: Be flexible and open to change. If a particular media type or strategy isn't working, don't hesitate to adapt and shift.

- Monitor And Adjust: Adopt a continuous learning approach by consistently monitoring and tweaking your strategy based on user engagement metrics.

- Use Platforms Effectively: Each social media platform has a different audience and preferred content type. Use this knowledge to tailor your multimedia content delivery accordingly.

8.5. Case Study: Using Multimedia For Effective Communication

Let's consider the example of a fictitious nonprofit, Child Aid Foundation which supports children's education. They wanted to increase their donations and visibility, and turned to multimedia communication.

They created a heartrending video showing the daily struggles of their beneficiaries and the positive impact of their work. The video, shared on their website and social channels, significantly boosted donations, shares, likes, and comments.

Next, they rolled out audio podcasts featuring interviews with beneficiaries and project heads, shedding more light on their work. They maintained a blog replete with text and images telling unique stories from the field. Consistent and quality communication helped them gain more loyalty, donations, and reach.

8.6. Conclusion

Embracing multimedia communication can provide nonprofits with an arsenal of tools and strategies to connect with their current audience and reach new ones. It's not just about using different forms of media, but blending them to narrate a compelling story that aligns with the organization's mission and resonates with the audience. It's high time nonprofits harnessed the power of multimedia communication to take their mission from conception to execution. In the digital era, an organization that cannot communicate effectively is one that cannot make a significant impact. Hence, creating and implementing a solid multimedia communication strategy is no longer an option but a necessity.

Chapter 9. Design Thinking in Nonprofit Communication

Design thinking is a highly iterative process that seeks to understand the user, challenge assumptions, and redefine problems, with a goal to identify alternative strategies that might not be immediately apparent. Its methodologies are particularly effective in settings where the problem is ill-defined or unknown, making it an incredibly relevant tool for nonprofit communication.

9.1. Understanding Design Thinking

Design thinking is fundamentally about empathy, a key component for any nonprofit organization. It challenges you to step into the shoes of your stakeholders - be they the community you serve, your volunteers, or your donors - to truly understand their needs, motivations, and expectations.

It involves five key stages: Empathizing, Defining, Ideologizing, Prototyping, and Testing. However, these stages are not sequential. Rather, they are meant to be undertaken iteratively until the best solution is found.

9.2. Applying Design Thinking to Nonprofit Communication

The application of design thinking in nonprofit communication enhances understanding of the target audiences, ensuring more effective communication and fostering deep connections. In fact, the significant majority of nonprofits that use design thinking find measurable improvement in their engagement and fundraising efforts.

Following the five stages of design thinking, you can adapt your communication strategy in a way that it resonates more powerfully with your audience:

1. *Empathize*: Spend time with your audience to understand their aspirations, challenges, and needs. This is achieved through surveys, interviews, and immersion in their environment. The insights you gain will provide a solid foundation for your communication.

2. *Define*: Synthesize your audience insights into an actionable problem statement. For example, "We need to communicate our mission in a way that emotionally engages our audience and inspires them to take action."

3. *Ideate*: Brainstorm a wide range of creative solutions. During this phase, aim for quantity over quality, as this helps stimulate innovative ideas.

4. *Prototype*: Develop low-fidelity versions of your solutions and share them with a small segment of your audience for feedback. This may involve drafting different versions of a donor appeal letter or designing mock-ups of your website.

5. *Test*: Refine your solutions based on what you learned from your prototype phase. Aim to make your communications more effective and engaging, ground on the feedback and reactions.

9.3. Leveraging Technology in Design Thinking

Today, technology presents vast opportunities for nonprofits to leverage design thinking in their communication strategy. Digital platforms make it easier to gather inputs from audiences and stakeholders, co-create solutions, and adapt communications in real time.

Social media networks allow organizations to initiate dialogues and get immediate feedback. Email marketing platforms provide significant data on recipients' behavior, giving insights into what resonates with the audience. Systems like customer relationship management (CRM) tools track donor behavior over time and serve as a knowledge base for understanding audience dynamics.

9.4. Case Study: An Example of Design Thinking in Action

To illustrate design thinking in action, consider the case of a nonprofit dedicated to sea turtle conservation. The organization needed to increase donations to fund their work.

In the Empathize stage, they reach out to current and potential donors to understand them better. Through surveys and conversations, they learn that while the donors find the cause crucial, they struggle to see the tangible impact of their donations.

In the Define stage, they reformulate their communication problem: "How can we show donors the direct effect their contribution has on sea turtle conservation?"

During Ideation, the team comes up with several solutions. They settle on illustrating stories of specific sea turtles that were helped through the fund.

In the Prototype stage, they create multiple versions of the stories to share with a small group of donors. They collect feedback and find that donors prefer real-life stories paired with photos and updates.

Finally, in the Test stage, they implement the changes in their communication and track donor responses through their CRM.

In conclusion, nonprofits that adopt design thinking in their communication strategy can create more potent messages that resonate with their audience. This not only increases engagement but also contributes to the effectiveness of the organization's mission. By spending the time to understand and empathize with their audience, defining clear communication goals, ideating innovative solutions, prototyping, and testing these solutions, nonprofit organizations can make a significant impact in their field.

Chapter 10. Building Community Relations: Partnerships for Greater Impact

One of the most potent tools in a nonprofit's arsenal is the cultivation of strategic relationships within the community. Strong bonds with locals, other nonprofits, businesses, and government entities not only amplify the organisation's voice but also expand resources and facilitate reciprocal support. These partnerships function as a robust support network for achieving shared objectives and ensuring sustainable growth.

10.1. Establishing Local Partners

Harnessing the power of place is integral to community-based nonprofits. Organizations must be knowledgeable and respectful of the locale, its culture, and traditions. Begin by fostering relationships with local influencers and stakeholders, such as community leaders, business owners, educational institutions, and even households. By doing so, you can incorporate local knowledge, skills, and resources toward strengthening your operations and programs.

Creating a 'Local Partnership Council' composed of representatives from various community sectors can streamline this process. The council can provide invaluable insights into the community's needs and existing resources, facilitate collaborative projects, and help diversify your organization's funding sources. Frequent town hall meetings can also allow direct interaction and engagement with locals, imparting a sense of ownership and personal investment in your organization's mission.

10.2. Collaboration with Other Nonprofits

Nonprofit collaboration is a symbiotic relationship where organizations work together to maximize their impact by sharing knowledge, skills, and resources. Rather than see each other as competitors, nonprofits that view each other as partners can create a significant collective impact in the community.

Formal agreements such as Memoranda of Understanding (MoU) can be used to outline the terms and conditions of the partnership. Nonprofits can also form networks or consortia to coordinate services, jointly fundraise, and share expertise. Regular interaction through joint events, workshops, and meetings strengthens these ties and encourages knowledge sharing.

10.3. Engaging Businesses in CSR Initiatives

Corporate Social Responsibility (CSR) is a practice where businesses commit to making a positive social impact. Nonprofits can tap into this by establishing partnerships with corporations looking to fulfill their CSR duties. In return, nonprofits get financial assistance, volunteers, and potential access to the company's network of contacts.

Start by identifying potential partners whose CSR goals align with your mission. Pitch your collaboration as a win-win situation, highlighting the mutual benefits. Remember, good relationship management is critical. Keep transparent communication, regularly update corporate partners on project progress, and acknowledge their contributions.

10.4. Building Relationships with Government Entities

Government entities are powerful allies for nonprofits, offering potential funding, legislative advocacy, resources, and platform to voice concerns. Start by identifying the government departments, agencies, or local councils aligned with your mission. Attend public meetings, voice your concerns, propose solutions, and express your interest in a partnership.

Nonprofits can also leverage government grants, loans, and programs that offer financial assistance. In exchange, nonprofits can offer their expertise and resources to help governments address social issues more effectively.

10.5. Leveraging Digital Platforms for Collaboration

In the digital era, nonprofits must effectively utilize online platforms for building stronger connections. Social media, virtual meetings, and email are invaluable tools for maintaining relationships with community stakeholders. Online platforms also provide nonprofits the power to bring together diverse stakeholders – from international donors to local volunteers – forging partnerships that were once limited by geographical boundaries.

10.6. Navigating Challenges in Building Community Relationships

Remember, building community relationships is not without its challenges. Potential obstacles may include conflicting objectives, miscommunication, mistrust, or imbalance of power. To navigate these difficulties, maintain open lines of communication, regularly review and renegotiate terms of partnerships, foster an environment of trust, and ensure all parties feel equally valued and heard.

10.7. Case Study: Community Coalition 'X'

To illustrate these strategies' effectiveness, let's examine the actions of nonprofit Community Coalition 'X'. It cultivated relationships with local leaders and businesses, formed a cooperative arrangement with like-minded nonprofits, engaged in CSR initiatives with tech companies, and engaged government entities for policy advocacy. The result was an extensive network of allies, financial resources, volunteers, and knowledge to run its programs effectively. 'X' demonstrated the compelling advantage of building community relations for a nonprofit's success.

In conclusion, building community relationships is a mutually beneficial strategy that enhances a nonprofit's operations, programming, and impact. By cultivating these relationships proactively, your nonprofit can build a strong support network, diversify its resources, and amplify its voice for change. Here's to making your mission possible through strategic community partnerships!

Chapter 11. Evaluating Your Communication Strategy: Tools and Techniques for Nonprofits

Understanding and improving your nonprofit's communication strategy is not a one-time endeavor but an ongoing process. Effective evaluation is instrumental in understanding the effectiveness of your communication efforts and in making necessary improvements. This section delves into several tools and techniques nonprofits can utilize to comprehensively evaluate and fine-tune their communication strategy.

11.1. The Importance of Evaluation

Evaluation is essential in assessing the effectiveness of your communication strategy. It provides data-backed insights outlining what works well and what needs revision. Evaluating your strategy helps you understand your audience better, improve your messaging, and ultimately, make a greater impact. By efficiently allocating resources and focusing on strategies that work, you can enhance your organization's reach and impact.

11.2. Key Performance Indicators (KPIs)

Key Performance Indicators (KPIs) are an excellent tool to measure the effectiveness of your communication strategy. KPIs are specific, measurable outcomes that indicate the success or failure of a task or project. If you're not meeting your KPIs, it's a signal that your strategy may need adjustments.

In the context of communication strategy, KPIs may include, but aren't limited to:

- External engagement: including social media likes, shares, comments, website visits, and email opens.

- Event turnout: counting how many people came to an event or how many viewed it online.

- Donations: tracking financial contributions, divided by size and frequency.

- Member or volunteer recruitment: counting the number of people who join or offer to help your cause.

11.3. Surveys

Conducting surveys is an effective way to assess the clarity and effectiveness of your communication strategies. Surveys can be carried out through various channels such as email, social media, or face-to-face during events.

Here are some questions that may be included in your survey:

- How clear and understandable is our message?

- How would you rate the relevance of our content to our cause?

- How effectively are we communicating the impact of our work?

- What are some areas where you feel our communication can improve?

11.4. A/B Testing

A/B testing, also known as split testing, involves two variants of a single variable to determine which performs better. The variants (A and B) are presented to users at random, and statistical analysis is used to determine which variant is more effective.

In terms of communication strategy, A/B testing could involve creating two different email newsletters or social media posts and measuring which version gets more engagement.

11.5. Social Media Metrics

With most nonprofits using social media to reach their audience, understanding social media analytics is crucial. Most social media platforms provide useful metrics that can help you evaluate your strategy.

Some key metrics to focus on are:

- Reach: The number of people who see your content.
- Engagement: The number of likes, comments, shares, and retweets your content receives.
- Click-Through-Rate (CTR): The number of people who click on your links relative to the number of total viewers.

11.6. Google Analytics

Google Analytics is a potent tool that helps track and report website traffic. It provides valuable insights about who is visiting your website, what they're doing while there, and where they're leaving.

For example, if many visitors leave your donation page without contributing, you might need to simplify your donation process or make your call to action clearer.

11.7. Feedback Sessions

Organizing feedback sessions with your supporters can provide qualitative insights about your communication strategy. Personal interactions can offer a wealth of information that surveys or analytics cannot.

During these sessions, encourage participants to share their thoughts about your messaging, communication channels, frequency of communication, etc. Be open to their feedback and responsive to their concerns or suggestions.

Understanding the effectiveness of your communication strategy and making necessary improvements is not an easy task. However, by investing in evaluation and leveraging tools and techniques like KPIs, surveys, A/B testing, social media metrics, Google Analytics, and feedback sessions, nonprofits can enhance their communication for optimum impact. Remember, communication is the heart of your nonprofit and, when done effectively, has the power to transform your organization's reach and mission impact.

www.ingramcontent.com/pod-product-compliance
Lightning Source LLC
Chambersburg PA
CBHW062308290526
45794CB00006B/2728